Communication

How to Communicate and Speak Effectively to Improve Your Influence, Public Speaking, Listening, and Social Skills for Beginners

by

Shea Hendricks

© 2016

Table of Contents

Introduction

So, you want to be a great public speaker? I'm sure people will have told you that great speakers are born, not made, and it is difficult not to believe that it's true. When you watch the best speakers they look comfortable, confident and natural in front of an audience, on the other hand, you don't feel confident on stage at all! You usually feel so nervous that you're drenched in sweat just at the thought of your next presentation.

Thankfully, great speakers aren't naturally born as great speakers - great speakers are made through preparation, practise and lots of hard work. If you want to see an example of how much hard work it takes to look comfortable and confident on stage, then you need to watch Jerry Seinfeld's movie "Comedian." Stand-up comics appear to be the most self-assured people in the world, but when they first get on stage to practise their jokes they can look just as awkward as the rest of us feel!

I want to let you into a secret, too – it is OK to feel nervous before you get on stage. Inside the book, I will explain to you WHY people feel nervous when they are speaking in front of an audience. But even the best speakers get nervous before they get in front of an audience, so don't worry if you are quivering with fear before you get on stage – you'll learn during the book how to deal with that fear so that no-one else can tell how nervous you are!

Finally, throughout the book I will refer to your public speeches as "presentations." The tips included throughout the book work as well for a best man's speech as they do for a TED talk. "Presentation" just felt like the best word to describe a speech in front of an audience.

So, before I get started with the first chapter of the book, I'm going to give you the most important piece of information in the whole book – you must put the tips in this book into action. If you don't put the tips into action, then you will not gain any benefit from the book!

At the end of each chapter I have put "next steps" for you to follow, make sure you put these steps into action and you will find your public speaking ability improve incredibly quickly.

Without any further adieu... let's get started!

Chapter 1 - Prepare!

One of the most common reasons for nerves is the feeling of being unprepared. I always like to say that perfect preparation makes for a perfect presentation!

If you don't feel prepared for a presentation, there will always be a nagging voice in the back of your head reminding you that you might forget your words or you might not know the answer to a question someone could ask you. The worst thing is that when your brain starts thinking about any outcome, the chances are that the outcome is exactly what will happen!

You definitely don't want to be thinking negative thoughts because they will end up becoming a self-fulfilling prophecy. If you're going to make something a self-fulfilling prophecy (and you usually will!) you want to make it something positive, and the good news is that the more you prepare, the less negative thoughts you will have.

They don't care about what you say, they care about who you are!

One of the most important parts of your presentation is the introduction. If the audience don't know you, then you need to demonstrate to your audience why they should listen to you during the introduction.

Why is that so important? It's important because most audience members will switch off during the first 10 minutes of your presentation. If you don't hook your audience straight away then you are risking losing most of the room, and believe me – it's easier to keep someone's attention than it is to win it back!

So the first thing you need to do is prepare a great introduction – you need to prepare something that you can stand on stage and confidently deliver. The introduction needs to include the following information – your name, what you are going to teach them, why you are qualified to teach them and why it is important for them to learn it.

The best way to put the information across to them is in the following format: "Hello, my name is *YOUR NAME* and today I am going to teach you the *WHAT YOU'RE GOING TO TEACH*. I am a *WHAT YOU DO* and I want to make sure that you can use these techniques to *WHY THEY NEED IT*."

The "what you're going to teach" needs to get your audience's interest straight away. You don't just want to tell them what it is you are going to teach, you want to tell them what they can do with it. For example, I wouldn't say "I am going to teach you about public speaking," because that's boring and not going to capture your interest at all. I would say "I am going to teach you the best way to overcome your fear of public speaking so that you can give powerful presentations."

Using words like "the best way to," "the seven proven ways you can" or "the secret of" will help gain your audience's interest quicker, too.

When you tell people what you do, you want to tell the audience how what you do, will help them. So I wouldn't just say "I give presentations," what I would say is "I use my vast experience in public speaking to help other people overcome stage fright." So rather than just "I do this," you're saying "because I do this, you gain this." By giving your audience that benefit, you can make the benefit into something they can see, once they can see what the benefit is to them they will be more likely to listen to you.

Finally, when you say why they need it you can paint a picture for the audience of what they can do with it, and you have the opportunity to dazzle the audience by demonstrating what you know. You can dazzle them by using a statistic that backs up the reason they need to learn what you're going to teach. So, something like "are you one of the 80% of people who suffer from stage fright? If so then you can use these techniques to get rid of stage fright forever!"

Once you've finished the introduction, you can split your presentation into different sections to cover the subjects that you want to teach your audience. The way you want to prepare you presentation is:

Introduction

Section 1

Section 2

Section 3 (and so on, as many sections as you need)

Conclusion

So right at the end you want to tie up your presentation with a conclusion. The conclusion will cover everything that your audience have learnt throughout the presentation and tell them the next steps for them to use the techniques you've taught them in the future.

Know how you will enter the stage!

Most people make the mistake of only preparing the words that they're going to speak. Which is good, but you'd don't just want to prepare your words - you want to prepare as much as you possibly can.

One of the most confident speakers I've ever known was a master of preparation, whenever he arrived at a venue the first thing he would do was plan his entrance to the stage. If he were walking to the back of the room, he would plan his route to the stage step by step.

Why?

Because the people usually make up their mind about someone within the first 30 seconds of seeing them. By plotting out his route to the stage step by step, he knew that he could walk to the stage with confidence which is projected to the audience.

Most people don't bother planning their route to the stage and then find that the room is set up in a very awkward fashion. That means the time the audience sees them they see someone who nervously has to shuffle between the tables, taking way too long to get up to the stage... do you think this first impression is positive?

This is just an example of how deep your preparation can go; it can extend to testing the microphone (if you're using one) and testing different lighting if you're on a big stage.

The rule of thumb is – if you can prepare it... then make sure you do prepare it.

You'll probably find that there is very little that you can't prepare for, some things that seem impossible to prepare for at first glance are really easy to prepare.

Make them ask questions!

Something that I have been asked on a number of occasions is "how do you prepare for questions at the end of your presentation?" If you are delivering training, this is one of those things that you just have to do, and it seems like something that's almost impossible to prepare for.

Think about it - the audience could ask practically anything, and for that reason many new speakers that I talk to try to avoid asking questions... which is a bad idea! If you don't give the audience a chance to ask you questions, you risk them going home unsatisfied, and you deprive yourself of the opportunity to find something that you can add to your presentation.

But, it is very easy for you to prepare for it, and I'm going to give you two ways that you can prepare for it.

The first one is for you if you have given a lot of presentations in the past or if you have access to the list of people who are coming to see you speak. If you can email the people that are coming, or if you can email people who have been to see you in the past – send them an email simply asking "What is the main thing that you want to learn/you wished you had learned from the presentation." This helps you because you can prepare to answer these questions throughout the presentation or, if you aren't planning on covering this in your presentation, you can prepare in case the question is asked.

If you don't have access to a list of people attending then get people to fill in a quick questionnaire when they come into the venue asking them the same question. Of course, this doesn't give you as much time to prepare but will give you an idea of what people might ask and you will have time to find answers which you can write down for them.

Something you will find when you have given a lot of presentations is that 90% of the questions asked will be the same across the board. So after a while you will be prepared for any questions that people will throw at you.

What If I Don't Have Time to Prepare?

If you are offered a presentation at short notice, or if you are going to turn up late to the venue then you aren't going to be able to prepare for everything. You might not have time to plan your route to the microphone, you probably won't be able to get answers to all of your questions and you might not have a chance to check the lighting. But you can still do some things to make sure you get yourself prepared.

The most important thing to do in these situations is to do whatever you can to get yourself comfortable on stage as quickly as possible. The time that you feel most nervous is at the beginning of your presentation, so what you need to do is focus on getting the beginning of your presentation well prepared. If you are pressed for time make sure that you practise the introduction and the first section of your presentation over and over again.

Once you've got through the first section of your presentation successfully you will feel more comfortable, and you will feel better about the rest of the presentation.

This will also work when you have a long presentation, and it's difficult to practise all of it.

What to do after the introduction?

The first thing you need to do is write a strong introduction and make sure you can deliver it in a confident manner. Once you've done that, arrange the rest of your presentation so that you have it separated into different subjects.

Once you've arranged your presentation into the right structure, then you can start practising it until you are comfortable with the presentation. Even if you are going to use cue cards, you want to know it inside out. The better you know it – even if you are using cue cards – the more comfortable you will feel on stage.

If you are speaking on stage tonight, then try getting there a little a bit earlier. Try planning your walk to the stage and testing out the microphone. Once you feel the benefit of the extra preparation you won't want to go back your old pre-presentation routine!

Chapter 2 – Visualize!

There was once a boxer who had a fight for the World Title, only half of the tickets for the fight were sold, and his opponent was a strong favourite. Against all expectations, he won the fight and today, this boxer is known as one of the best boxers of all time!

If that seems like a very random story that has no part to play in the book, you're wrong! The boxer was Muhammad Ali, and a lot of his success was down to visualization techniques. The techniques were almost unknown in the 1960's and 1970's, but they have become commonplace today with sportspeople, and there's a good reason for that – they work!

Muhammed Ali called the technique that he used "future history" and he used it throughout his career to help him win fight after fight. This is a technique you can use to help you to help make every one of your presentations successful.

Make use of the "Future History"!

Future history is a visualization technique you use to see your outcome in an incredibly positive manner. Ali called it future history because he would visualise the future as though it had already happened.

"Creative visualization," as it is usually called, has been used by athletes, celebrities and businesspeople to help them achieve success. As well as Muhammad Ali, other people who have attributed their success to these techniques such as Tiger Woods, Bill Gates and Arnold Schwarzenegger.

The reason why these techniques work so well is that when your brain can actually "see" an outcome, it does everything in its power to make it happen again. As I explained in the last section - if you see negative outcomes you will have negative experiences – it becomes a self-fulfilling prophecy. On the other hand, if you see a positive outcome then you will have positive experiences.

Some of you might be reading that section and wondering why I used the words "happen again." You might be thinking "how can it happen again when it hasn't really happened in real life." That is where the real power of these techniques comes into play. Although you know that the experience has only happened in your mind, not in real life, your brain cannot tell the difference between imagined and reality.

Think about the last time that you did something embarrassing and remember how that made you feel.

Did you really feel the urge to cringe and did that feeling of absolute embarrassment come back to you? For most people, it does, and that is because your brain cannot tell whether you imagined the embarrassing experience or if it actually experienced it. Your brain gives you the same physical response whether it is real or not.

So when you imagine going into the future and seeing the positive outcome, your brain believes it has already happened, and you get the positive feelings associated with it. This gives you more positive feelings when you get up on stage for real and, because your brain believes it has happened once, it does everything possible to make it happen again.?

Is There Any Proof That Visualization Has Worked?

Yes, a study carried out by Australian psychologist Alan Richardson took three groups of Basketball players and separated them into three groups. Group 1 practised free throws for 20 minutes each day; group 2 did nothing at all, and group 3 visualized practising free throws but did not take any real free throws.

The outcome was astounding – group 1 had a significant improved (no surprise), group 2 had no significant improvement (no surprise), but group 3 had a significant improvement which was almost as dramatic as group 1!

This is an incredible finding when it comes to public speaking – because one of the big problems with getting enough practise in front of an audience is that you need to have an audience to speak to.

Sometimes that can be difficult, sure you can join speaking groups (and I recommend you do) but it is said that you need to get 10,000 hours of practise to become an expert at something.

To become an expert public speaker, you would need to speak for an hour a day for over 27 years!

Most of us won't have the opportunity to speak in front of an audience every single day and, while we can benefit from practising in front of a mirror, that experience pales in comparison to the experience gained by standing in front of an audience.

Visualization techniques will allow you to take a short-cut towards becoming an expert by allowing you to gain the experience in your mind whenever you don't have the opportunity to speak in front of an audience.

The Best Way to Benefit From Visualization!

There are two great techniques you can use to benefit from visualization:

The first way is to use future history to give you the confidence boost when your brain sees something happen. This will boost your confidence and get your brain looking to make the positive outcome a "self-fulfilling prophecy."

The second way is to use "mental practise" to visualize yourself doing something. That way you can pull yourself closer to the 10,000-hour mark even though you can't find a way to speak in front of a real audience.

The more often you do this, the more effective it becomes. So, even if you can only commit to taking half an hour or an hour a day to follow these visualization techniques – doing them regularly will give you a massive boost to your confidence and ability.

How to Carry Out the Future History Technique.

To do future history, you need to sit in a room where you won't be disturbed, close your eyes and picture a future where you have just finished an incredibly successful presentation.

See it from an observer, how does it look when you have finished the speech. How happy do you look? What can you see around you? How do the other people look?

Then think about the sounds, what can you hear? Are people clapping? Are they cheering? Is the audience giving you a standing ovation?

Also imagine the smell of the room, consider everything that you will smell to make the experience feel as real as possible.

Then move into your body and view it from your eyes – what do you see? How will it look through your eyes when you have finished the speech?

Most importantly, how do you feel? Are you excited?

Happy? Ecstatic? Proud?

Now, turn up the brightness in the picture, make all the colours as bright as you can. Turn up the volume, hear the clapping and cheering. Finally, turn up the feelings, this is the most important part – send that feeling all the way through your body and feel it as intensely as you can.

How did that feel? You should feel more excited about your next speech because this is the outcome that you are going to have once it has finished!

How to Carry Out Mental Practise.

To carry out mental practise, you need to sit in a room where you won't be disturbed, close your eyes and imagine you are in front of an audience. This will work best if you have a presentation prepared and you have practised the presentation to the point where you understand it without looking at the presentation itself. You do not need to practise the full presentation mentally, so if you have only prepared one section – that's fine, just practise that.

Firstly, you need to see everything through your own eyes – so look out into the audience, what do you see? Is it a big venue? Are the lights down? Can you see the full audience, the full row, or are the lights so bright that you can't see anyone!

Hear the clapping start to subside as you are on the stage ready to speak your first words. Then run through the full presentation in your mind as though you are performing it. Imagine it as though it is the perfect presentation – you get claps when you want the audience to clap; you get cheers when you want cheers, and you hear laughter when you tell a joke.

When you get to the end of the presentation, you want to imagine everything as you would in future history but see it all through your eyes. See, hear and feel everything that you would expect to feel after giving the presentation of your life!

How does that feel? The real benefit of this exercise will be felt when you get on stage for your next presentation. You will feel as though you have done this before, and you will feel more relaxed because, as far as your brain knows, the last time you did this it felt perfect!

If you have never given a presentation before then the mental practise will help you, but it will become more effective when you can fully understand how you will feel when you are on stage.

Next Steps

Your next step is to take the time to carry out these visualization techniques. Doing them once will help – but when you get into a routine of carrying out the techniques once or twice a day you will really start to notice its impact.

The sooner you try these techniques out, the quicker you will feel the benefit, and there's no time like the present.

So find a quiet place where you won't be disturbed and try these techniques out now – you won't regret it!

Chapter 3 – Relax!

Stage fright puts people in a horrible state of stress and nerves, and most of us suffer from it! Surveys about fears frequently place public speaking right at the top of the list, even above dying!

It doesn't seem logical to put public speaking at the top of the list when you think about it seriously. The long term implications of a bad speech is a little embarrassment, but the long term implication of dying is... well... dying!

But all of us, even the most confident and competent public speaker, have been frozen with fear at one point in our lives. There's good news for all of us though, scientists understand why people fear public speaking so much and, most importantly, it is possible to overcome the fear!

Why Do We Fear Public Speaking So Much?

The fear of public speaking comes from our ancient past and a time when embarrassment might have, in a roundabout way, led to death!

Humans have survived without being the fastest, largest or fiercest animal; our survival has relied upon being able to work together as part of a group. The importance of the group was especially great in the earliest time of our history.

If you had done something stupid in front of your peers at one time in our history (like, telling an ill-advised joke during a speech which offended your tribe leader) you may have ended up being kicked out of the group. Being kicked out of the group at that stage in our history didn't just mean that that you got a bit lonely and missed the company of your friends – it meant that you would be easy prey for other animals!

Being kicked out of a group in our early history would have almost certainly led to a very quick death!

The fear of being ostracised from society has become a fear ingrained in humans and for that reason we hold deep fears about doing anything that could risk our position in a social group. This is why people feel nervous when attending a job interview, going on a date or taking part in a sporting event. In ancient times failure and rejection could have had much more dire consequences than wanting to hide away from public for a few days!

How Do We Overcome This Fear?

I know, overcoming a fear that has been inside us for centuries seems almost impossible... but it's not! I don't want to make it sound too simple, but all you need to do is relax!

I know that sounds like telling you that to paint the Mona Lisa all you need is some paint and a canvas, but all you really need to do is relax. Being prepared and using visualization will help you to relax but there are more things that you can do to relax yourself before an important presentation.

The first thing you can do is speak to a couple of members of the audience before you start a presentation. Especially if it is a presentation where people have come specifically to see you. Walk up and sit next to them, say "hello" and introduce yourself. Find out their name, ask them some questions about themselves and sincerely listen to them. This will communicate to the audience member that you care about them, and this can help you before the presentation because you have already interacted with a member of the audience.

But, most importantly, it will help relax you during the presentation.

When you are in the middle of your presentation, you can look out to see the face of someone who you have spoken to beforehand. Looking out at a familiar face in the audience is a great way to help you relax, even if the familiar face is someone you only met 5 minutes before you walked up on stage!

Something that is important for you to remember is that it is OK to be nervous. Some of the best public speakers feel nervous every single time they step out on stage. The most important thing isn't to stop yourself feeling nervous – but to make sure that no matter how nervous you feel, the audience see someone who looks 100% confident!

I know that sounds a bit strange, but I'll explain it to you. If you feel so nervous that you want the ground to swallow you up before you step on stage, that isn't great – BUT if you get on stage and appear confident, then the audience will have a lot of confidence in you and they will listen to what you have to say.

If you feel incredibly nervous throughout your presentation but your audience thought you were a confident and charming speaker, and they took everything from your speech that you wanted to give them – does it really matter if you felt nervous all the way through?

The most important part of any presentation is the audience's perception of it. Many speakers will tell you that the moment you know you should quit isn't when you feel so nervous you want to throw up, it's when you don't feel nervous at all. Because the moment you don't feel nervous is also the moment that you won't feel excited, and if you don't feel excited then it's clearly not something that you want to do anymore!

If the tension is so high in your body that you are going to appear nervous to your audience, then you want to use a technique called "progressive relaxation." Progressive relaxation is a powerful technique that is similar to self-hypnosis and will help relax every single part of your body!

How to Use Progressive Relaxation!

Progressive relaxation is something that you can use at any time, and it will always have a positive effect on you because you can never be too relaxed!

For public speaking, you want to use progressive relaxation whenever you feel tension throughout your body. If you walk on stage with a lot of tension in your body, you will communicate to the audience that you are nervous with your body language. As we know, the perception of the audience is the most important thing for us, and we don't want the audience to have the impression that we are nervous.

Progressive relaxation is "progressive" because you work through all of your muscle groups relaxing them one by one. Progressive relaxation will help you feel more relaxed and look confident, too.

Progressive relaxation is something that you can do wherever you are. I would always recommend using a quiet room that you can lay down in, but it is possible to do it anywhere.

Focus on fully relaxing all of your muscles and clear your mind.

Start with your forehead and try to push your eyebrows up as high as they can go for 5 seconds and then relax them.

Close your eyes as tightly as possible and hold it for 5 seconds before relaxing them.

Pull your mouth into a grimace and hold it for 5 seconds before relaxing.

Hold your hands in a tight fist for 5 seconds before relaxing.

Push forward with your hands in front of your body for 5 seconds before relaxing.

Tense your biceps for 5 seconds before relaxing.

Push your shoulders up towards the ceiling for 5 seconds before relaxing.

Arch your back for 5 seconds before relaxing.

Tighten your abdomen for 5 seconds before relaxing.

Tighten your muscles around your hips and buttocks for 5 seconds before relaxing.

Press your legs together to tighten your thigh muscles for 5 seconds before relaxing.

Bend your ankles towards your body for 5 seconds before relaxing.

Curl your toes tightly for 5 seconds before relaxing.

Repeat the exercise for any areas of your body that are still tense until the muscles fully relax.

If you struggle to relax your mind fully, try and go somewhere a little quieter for a few minutes.

Next Steps

The next steps are to notice when you are feeling nervous and make sure that you remember that it is OK to feel nervous... some nervousness is healthy!

But make sure you recognize when your nervousness might hinder your performance and take the steps to relax yourself as much as possible when you are on stage. Make sure that your preparation is up to scratch and try to speak to at least one audience member before your presentation.

Chapter 4 – Laugh!

In this chapter, you'll find a two step stage fright buster! Laughter is a great way stress buster and for this reason laughing will make you feel a lot better about getting up on stage and speaking to an audience. Stress is also a great way to ease tension, and sometimes your audience will be just as nervous about your speech as you are! By making your audience laugh, you will ease their tension and relax them too, by relaxing your audience you will feel better about your speech too!

The most important thing to take away from this chapter is that you want to have fun whenever you're speaking in public. Take the time to have fun and enjoy yourself, by doing that you will encourage your audience to have fun too! The more fun you and your audience have, the better your presentation will be!

Making Yourself Laugh Will Help Your Stage Fright!

The biggest problem that many people have before they get on stage is that they spend their entire preparation time worrying about what could go wrong. As I've said a few times, the more you think about something happening – the more likely it is to happen!

We've spent time telling our brain how good we are at something by visualizing the most positive outcome. Before you go on stage, your mind will take one last opportunity to save you from the possible negative outcome. When you're at the venue waiting to give your presentation your mind will try screaming at you "watch, this might happen! Then you'll be an outcast... then you'll die!"

You can't reason with your mind and you might not have the time or space to sit in a quiet corner and run through positive visualizations, so what can you do?

The answer is very simple; the best thing you can do is distract your mind!

I'm assuming you've prepared fully; you've run through positive visualizations and you've run through some relaxation techniques. At this point, you want to keep your mind away from the thought of going on stage, and you want to keep it on happy thoughts.

Get YouTube up on your mobile and watch some funny videos, listen to your favourite comedian on your iPod or just think about funny things that have happened to you. Take the time to distract yourself from the presentation you have to give and just enjoy yourself for a few minutes.

You will feel a lot better afterwards for a few reasons: firstly, you will forget about the frightening thing coming up so you will feel a lot more relaxed, and secondly, you will release endorphins when you laugh which will fight off the stress hormones, relax you and make you feel happier.

Your Audiences' Laughter Will Improve Your Stage Fright!

At the beginning of any presentation, there will be tension in the room while the audience works out if you are any good or not. Most people will ignore the tension and just get on with their presentation, which does work – eventually! Some will comment on the tension, which is using a comic technique where you notice something that everyone has seen, and you make a comment on it – it's called "calling the room."

"Calling the room" can break the tension and help relax everyone – if you do it right. The comment needs to be delivered confidently; it must be funny and it must be appropriate! I use the example of tension in the room because it is something you can always expect to be able to comment on at the beginning of your presentation, but you can use this for anything. A technical fault or some weird fact about the venue can be used for comic effect.

Russell Brand made great use of "calling the room"

during his tour "Scandalous" in 2009. He had just been involved in a huge scandal after making some ill-judged phone calls on his radio show that caused huge offence. At the beginning of the show he asks the audience how much they paid for tickets and as soon as someone tells him he says "you paid 25 pounds, to come and see me? After what I've done!" The joke immediately relaxes the audience because he talks about something the whole audience is thinking.

One difficulty in using humour in a presentation is that you don't know if something will work until you say the joke. Professional comedians test and tweak their jokes over and over again until they are fully happy with it – and their jokes won't work all of the time. As you aren't a comedian you won't be judged to the same standards as someone like Jerry Seinfeld, but an ill-judged offensive or unfunny comment could still lose you the room!

The best technique I can give you to help you use humour is "rehearsed spontaneity." Rehearsed spontaneity gives the impression of being spontaneous when you deliver a comment that you have made hundreds of times before. This is used to great effect by a lot of the top comedians. Don't be fooled when you see a comedian who tells you "I was on my way to the venue when this happened," chances are that the event happened months or years ago, and it's "happened on the way to the venue" ever since!

Comedians make careers out of appearing to be spontaneous. Many of them do whatever they can to give the appearance of something coming to mind on the spot –

even if they deliver the same material night after night. They do this because the audience will usually be more impressed with an off the cuff comment than they will be if they know that you tell the joke all of the time. Plus, the expectation is a little bit lower if the audience believes you have just thought of it, so they will be more likely to laugh than if they think that you've spent hours crafting the perfect joke!

Of course, naturally coming up with hilarious spontaneous jokes when you're stood on stage. Even the most quick-witted, naturally funny of us will find that their mind goes blank when they need to come up with something funny in front of an audience. That is why you want to have some very well-prepared and rehearsed "spontaneous comments."

How to rehearse to be spontaneous.

You want to look at things that could be present in a room that you can comment on. There will always be tension in the room when you start your presentation, so this is something that you can use. Other things that you could use are empty seats, technical issues with your equipment or a comment people usually make when they first meet you.

The question you're probably asking is, "how do you

come up with jokes?" The good thing for you is that you are not a professional comedian so you will not be held to the same standards as someone who needs to be funny for a living. People look down on comedians for using "stock lines" or following old comedy joke structures, but you can get away with it.

"Stock lines" are lines that have been used by so many presenters or speakers that no-one owns them. You can use these without being called a "joke thief!" An example of one of a stock line is one that you can use when there's a lot of chairs empty, "I wish someone told me it was fancy dress, I especially like these guys – who've come dressed as empty chairs." It also applies to lines like "there hasn't been this much tension in the room since..." and adding an event that would be familiar to the audience. If you see the same line being used by lots of different speakers you can assume that it's OK to use. Err on the side of caution, though – you do not want to be known as a joke thief!

Comedy joke structures are easy ways of writing a joke. Many professional comedians won't use them because after they've been used a couple of times the audience pick up on the joke structure, and the technique loses its effectiveness. However, you can use it because you are not going to deliver an entire comedy set!

The first of the joke structures I'll describe is "the rule of 3," which involves you giving a list of 3 things. The first one introduces a theme, the second re-enforces that theme and the third one breaks it – and that's where you find the humour. A great example of a "rule of three" joke is the following line to a bald person from the Dick Van Dyke show, "Can I get you anything? Cup of coffee, Doughnut, Toupee?" You obviously don't want to say something that offends a member of the audience, but you can use this technique to make a similar joke about yourself, the room or your subject.

The second joke structure is a "pull back and reveal" joke. A pull back and reveal joke involves you telling a story but leaving out an import piece of information until right at the end of the joke. An example would be this joke by Les Dawson, "I took the wife's family out for tea and biscuits. They weren't too happy about having to give blood, though." The joke works because you imagine that Les Dawson has taken the family to a nice tea room, and it's only at the end of the joke that you find out that he really took them to give blood. If you were telling the story in the chronological order, it would be "I took the wife's family to give blood, then we had tea and biscuits," which isn't a very funny story!

To make the jokes seem spontaneous, you can say that it happened on the way to the venue. This makes the audience think that you're telling them something that just happened, and you didn't plan to tell them originally, or link the joke to something in the room.

You can simply say "I was on my way to the venue." A more effective method is to link it to something in the town so "I was outside of..." or "I was in the..." because it allows the audience to picture where you were, and the extra detail makes the story seem more believable.

You could also link the joke to something in the room, which is a lot more difficult because you may not see the room until you turn up to the venue for the first time. You don't just have to speak about physical things that you see in the room; you can talk about subjects that range from the atmosphere to the cost of attending. So, you want to use your jokes about tension in the room here because you will usually find tension in a room before you start your presentation.

Next Steps

The first step is to build a collection of jokes that you can use at the beginning of your presentation to help you and the audience relax. If you start by picking up a number of strong stock lines and attempt to write a few jokes using the structures explained in this chapter.

It's impossible to know how well a joke will work until you have tried it out in front of an audience. You can try your jokes out on friends and family members, but never tell them that you are trying out jokes for your presentation because you won't get a real response. You can also try them out on open mic comedy nights – this might be very nerve-racking for you, but you will find open mic comedy audiences to be very supportive of you. You can simply write down a list of jokes and read them out one by one. All you need is 5 minutes worth of jokes that you want to try out and then you can get on stage and try them out. Once you have the jokes that you know will work, you can put them into your presentation.

The next step is to subscribe to some YouTube channels that have funny videos and fill your iPod with comedy that you can watch before your next presentation. This way you will be prepared in case you start to get nervous when preparing for a presentation.

Chapter 5 – Posture!

As children we were always told "stand up straight" and "don't slouch." The underlying reason that we are told this is because our posture has a huge part to play in how confident we look and how confident we feel. Tests have shown a dramatic increase in the confidence of people when they take up a specific posture.

As a confident feeling and appearance is important when you are speaking then getting your posture right will improve your speaking ability dramatically.

Posture for Feeling Confident.

If you've never heard of "power poses" before then the information in this chapter will make a huge difference to your feelings of confidence on a day to day basis. Professor Amy Cuddy of Harvard Business School gave a TED talk called "your body language shapes who you are." The talk contained some amazing findings on how your body language could be making you more confident or more stressed!

The first amazing finding is that people who took up a "high power" posture for 2 minutes (e.g. stood straight, head straight ahead, feet shoulder length apart, shoulders open, hands on hips) found that their levels of testosterone rose by 20%!

Testosterone is a "dominance" hormone which is linked to confidence and motivation.

People who took up a "low power" posture for 2 minutes (slumped shoulders, looking down at the ground, feet and arms crossed) had a drop in testosterone by 10%.

The second finding was that the people who took up a "low power" posture had a rise in cortisol levels while the "high power" posture brought about a significant drop in cortisol levels.

Cortisol is a stress hormone. Lower levels of cortisol help you deal with stressful situations better, which is very useful when you about to step into a very stressful situation on stage!

As you can see, these changes came about with just 2 minutes of these poses – do you have 2 minutes spare before your next speech? I imagine you do! So find the time to stand straight, feet shoulder length apart, looking straight ahead, shoulders opened up and hands on your hips. The increase in confidence and reduction in stress will help you when you start your presentation.

Posture for Appearing Confident.

So much of our communication is non-verbal and nowhere is that more apparent than when you are in front of an audience. You are sending messages simply by the way that you stand. Many people who are delivering a speech for the first time use their arms as a barrier, which tells the audience that you aren't comfortable on stage or pace around which gives the impression that you simply can't wait to get out of there!

You want to give the audience the impression that you are comfortable and confident on stage. You want your audience to think that you want to be there and that they need to listen to you!

The best posture when you are speaking to an audience is simply to stand up straight which shows the audience that you are comfortable and confident. You should lean slightly forward to show that you care and bend your knees slightly, putting your weight on the balls of your feet to let you move with energy if you need to.

Standing with this posture will make sure that you appear confident during your presentation, no matter how nervous you might feel inside!

Next Steps

The first step is to try the power pose before your next presentation; this should help you feel a lot more relaxed and confident. If you have a spare 2 minutes every day, then you will notice big improvements in all areas of your life, not just on stage!

The next step is to use a video camera to film your presentation the next time you are in front of an audience.

Then you need to practise your posture for the stage, rehearse in front of the mirror standing as you would in front of an audience. You want to feel completely natural in that posture when you are in front of an audience.

Chapter 6 - Confidence!

Body language says so much before you even open your mouth. But, no matter how confident your body language is if you sound nervous and trip over words when you do speak then you will still appear nervous. Speaking confidently can be difficult, but there are things you can do to make your speaking sound completely confident.

Use these little tricks to make you sound, as well as look, confident.

Speak From Your Diaphragm.

If you've ever had singing lessons, then you'll know how important diaphragmatic breathing is. It is used to make sure that you don't keep gasping for air, which doesn't sound all that confident!

Diaphragmatic breathing helps you control your breath better, project your voice louder and it gives you an authoritative sound.

So how do you speak from your diaphragm?

It's incredibly easy; you can practise it now by laying down and putting a book on your stomach. Exhale fully and then inhale for a count of 5 to raise the book with your stomach, exhale again for a count of 5. If you've never carried out any breathing exercises before then you might have found this difficult, so practise this every single day.

The more you practise, the easier you will find it to speak from your diaphragm and the easier you will find it to control your breathing.

Speak Slower!

One of the biggest problems that people have when it comes to speaking in front of an audience is speeding up and speaking too quickly for the audience. There are a few reasons why people do this; one reason is that they aren't prepared well enough so they speak quickly because they're scared they'll forget the words. Another reason may be because they are nervous, so they automatically speed up their speaking rate.

Whatever the reason is, speaking quickly will make you look nervous and will usually mean that the audience members struggle to keep up with what you're saying. People can only take in information at the rate that they speak, so if you speed up too much you will lose a significant part of your audience.

A good rule of thumb is to force yourself to slow down your rate of speaking by 20% of what you think is a normal speaking rate. The reason to slow down that much is because what you think is a normal speaking rate usually sounds too fast when you listen back. Plus it will make you sound a lot more confident because confident speakers expect the audience to hang on their words – so they will usually speak extra slowly.

Preparing properly will help you speak at a slower rate and standing with the right posture will make you feel a lot more comfortable, which will help you feel more comfortable speaking slowly.

If you still feel like you will be talking too slowly then record yourself speaking 20% slower than your usual rate of speaking and listen to it back. When you're speaking, you will probably feel as though you are talking way too slowly, but once you listen to it back you'll be surprised how normal it sounds.

Stop Saying "Umm" and "Err".

Something that immediately marks you out as an unconfident speaker is the use of verbal ticks like "umm" and "err." If you are completely confident in yourself, you won't be scared of pausing when you think of the next thing you are going to say.

Unfortunately, most of us use these verbal ticks all of the time without thinking about it, even if we feel confident. Even if you can't train them out of your everyday speaking, you want to work hard to train them out of any presentations you do. Great preparation will help with this as you are more likely to say "err" if you forget what you are meant to say next.

Try and get comfortable with silence when you are speaking by purposely including pauses during your presentation. If you know that silence is OK it will be easier to leave a pause when you are thinking of words to say. It is also worth recording parts of your presentation and listening back to see if you use these verbal ticks without thinking, once you know about them you can start eliminating them.

Next Steps

Practise diaphragmatic breathing on a daily basis, getting your breathing right will help give you a more powerful voice which will improve your speaking dramatically. Record and listen to yourself speaking 20% slower than usual so that you can hear how natural it sounds to speak at that rate. Finally, include silences in your speeches so you can feel comfortable with silence when you re speaking and start to eliminate verbal ticks from your presentations.

Chapter 6 - What The Best Speakers Do AFTER Their Presentation?

So, you have finished your presentation, and you're feeling over the moon or disappointed with how it went – either way, your work doesn't stop there!

As soon as you leave the stage for one presentation, your thoughts need to be on your next presentation! As I mentioned earlier it takes 10,000 hours of practise to become an expert at something, so you want to be speaking in front of audiences as often as possible.

Review Your Performance.

The first thing you want to do when you have come down from the high of your performance is to look back through the presentation and see what went well and what you can improve on. Especially watch out for moments where you look or sound nervous and parts of the presentation that can be better prepared.

Take notes as you watch it back and look at ways you can improve next time. For example, if you have an almost perfect performance but you stutter or say "umm" a lot during one section then you know that you need to rehearse that section again. On the other hand, if your posture is poor and this makes you look nervous throughout the presentation then you know where you need to focus on for next time.

Get Up On Stage Again.

The best way to become good at something is to do it as often as possible! So aim to speak in front of audiences regularly. If you don't have regular work lined up then a great way to guarantee a regular audience is to join a group like Toastmasters.

Toastmasters are a group who meet to improve communication and public speaking skills. Joining a group like this will allow you to speak in front of an audience regularly who can support you and give you constructive advice to help you improve. If you don't have a Toastmasters group nearby – consider setting one up.

Don't underestimate how dramatic your improvements will be if you regularly speak in front of an audience. By getting in front of an audience regularly, you can take issues that you've had in the most previous performance and improve on them immediately. The other big benefit is that you can tweak certain parts of your presentation or change the wording in certain sections to test what works best, which is very difficult to do if you only speak once every few months.

Seek Constructive Advice.

Sometimes you need someone else to give you advice because it is difficult for you to view your work from someone else's perspective. You could invite someone to watch you and ask for their advice afterwards, or you can send a video of it to them someone.

You can always ask a friend, but it is always worth asking someone completely impartial because a friend may not want to hurt your feelings by telling you something you might not want to hear.

Make sure you take the advice on board and don't take it personally. Remember that if there is something that you are doing wrong – it's better to know about it so that you can change it.

Next Steps

Consider joining a group like Toastmasters, most local Toastmasters groups will allow you to attend the first session for free before you choose to join the group. Seek advice from people as often as you can do, joining a group like Toastmasters will make finding that advice easy, as people within the group may offer it without you needing to ask for it. If not then consider inviting a friend/family member to watch you speak, or send a video of it to someone who's opinion you would respect.

Record and review every single presentation you give afterwards. Prepare to improve on any issues you see before your next presentation.

Finally, and most importantly, keep your diary full! Aim to speak a number of times every single week, joining a group like Toastmasters will help you with that. The more often you can speak in front of an audience, the more comfortable you will feel and the quicker you will improve.

Conclusion

Public speaking is something that frightens everyone, and you deserve respect for choosing to put yourself in front of an audience.

By now you will understand that the most important thing is to appear confident and that no matter how nervous you feel. As long as the audience think the presentation was great then how you felt doesn't matter!

Now that you have the knowledge, you need to put it into practise. So many people read through a book and never use any of the tips included inside, don't be one of those people! Use the visualization techniques and use the other tips to help you prepare. Follow all of the tips and tricks laid out in the book because they work!

If you're like me, you'll probably think that the information is great but in a couple of days you'll look for another book to learn more and then another one to learn even more. What you'll find if you do this is that your knowledge improves, but your ability doesn't!

It's important to remember that knowledge has never made a great speaker, action is what will make you a great speaker. Preparing, performing, reviewing and repeating the cycle is what will turn you into a great speaker.

So, take action and follow the tips outlined in the book, and you will see dramatic improvements!

Thank you for reading and happy public speaking!

www.ingramcontent.com/pod-product-compliance
Lightning Source LLC
Chambersburg PA
CBHW071827200526
45169CB00018B/1155

* 9 7 8 1 5 3 3 4 7 3 8 8 2 *